Klein's Handicapping Systems

By Robert Klein

BRIEF HISTORY

I have been enjoying thoroughbred and standardbred racing for the last twenty years. In the last five years my wife and I have concentrated on developing our own techniques for selecting winners. As you have already learned in our introduction, we have been successful beyond our wildest expectations.

I have been in private business for the last twenty-three years. It is a full-time job, and has limited my time at the race track. With our horse racing system improving each season, we hope soon to devote more time developing further techniques and just being at the track.

We apply our handicapping system to both thoroughbred and standardbred racing. So that there is no confusion, all the following calculations will be done on standardbred races.

PROOF OF SYSTEM

AMOUNT WAGERED ON OUR NINE SUPERSIX WINS

Bet >>>>>>>>>>>>>>>>>>>>>> **Payout**

$54.00————————————————-—$3096.00

$24.00————————————————-—$3096.00

$16.00————————————————-—$8837.00

$24.00————————————————-—$141.00

$48.00————————————————-—$2008.00

$32.00————————————————-—$550.00

$24.00————————————————-—$17,931.00

$32.00————————————————-—$443.00

$96.00————————————————-—$19,750.00

The first two payments are identical because I made up a bet for friends from out of town. When it came time to bet, they decided the SuperSix was too difficult a wager and did not want to participate. I had already made my own bet for $54.00 and did not plan on spending any more money on the SuperSix, but seeing as I had spent all this time constructing this bet I decided to go for both bets myself. You can imagine the look on everyone's faces when both tickets were winners.

The bet for $96.00 is definitely not our usual amount. In this case there was a three-day carryover (no one had won the SuperSix for 3 days). The pool was now at 220,000.00. I had made a bet for $48.00, but in the final adjustments I needed one more horse which doubledourbet price. Needless to say , he won. We were one of eleven winning tickets that evening which paid a handsome $19,750.00.

Aagje and I do not know any jockeys, trainers, or owners of horses. We do not use computers, expensive calculators or any other such devices. Our system is simple and straightforward. All of our information comes solely from the RACING FORM. We certainly do not pretend to know all the answers, but we are willing to share with you the ones that work for us. Maybe, if we combine our knowledge we can all move one step closer to achieving our mutual goal of picking every winner.

WINNING CHEQUES NEXT ....

PHOTOCOPIES OF SOME OF OUR WINNING CHEQUES
★ ★ ★ ★ ★ ★ ★ ★ ★ ★ ★ ★ ★ ★ ★ ★ ★ ★ ★ ★

CLOVERDALE RACEWAY — No. 1028
Dec 19 86
PAY TO THE ORDER OF Robert Klein — $2008 40
Two Thousand Eight
FOR TAB
CANADIAN IMPERIAL BANK OF COMMERCE

CLOVERDALE RACEWAY — No. 5934
Mar 13 86
PAY TO THE ORDER OF Robert Klein — $17,600 00
Seventeen Thousand Six Hundred
FOR HP
CANADIAN IMPERIAL BANK OF COMMERCE

CLOVERDALE RACEWAY — No. 0868
Mar 29 84
PAY TO THE ORDER OF Robert Klein — $8,837 00
Eighty Eight Hundred Thirty Seven
FOR PB
CANADIAN IMPERIAL BANK OF COMMERCE

THE BRITISH COLUMBIA JOCKEY CLUB
MUTUELS ACCOUNT — No. 2039
25 Mar 1986
PAY TO THE ORDER OF Robert Klein — $19,750 00
THE TORONTO-DOMINION BANK
THE BRITISH COLUMBIA JOCKEY CLUB

AMOUNT WAGERED ON OUR NINE SUPERSIX WINS

Having moved from Vancouver, British Columbia to the smaller city of Kelowna in the same province we found ourselves with no race track around. No more horse racing for the next five years! But all was not lost in our relocation wager, as after that five years a province wide horse race competition was announced. I said to my wife, let's enter. We had to handicap eleven races. A horse that wins gets you 5 points, a horse finishing second gets you 3 and a third place pick gives you 1 point. I had six winners, three picks in second and one horse finishing third. That totalled 40 points and my wife scored 39 points. We received a letter that I had won the contest. And a dinner for two at the Cloverdale Raceway.

DINNER FOR TWO LETTER NEXT ...

CLOVERDALE RACEWAY
17755 - 60TH AVENUE,
SURREY, B.C. V3S 1V3
TELEPHONE (604) 576-9141
FAX (604) 576-9821

SANDOWN HARNESS RACEWAY
BOX 2370, SIDNEY, B.C. V8L 3Y3
TELEPHONE (604) 656-1631
FAX (604) 656-7422

Congratulations!!

You have won "Dinner for Two" in the fabulous, "All You Can Eat" Clubhouse Buffet at Cloverdale Raceway.

This prize is awarded in honor of your 'topping the list of winners' in the AirBC Harness Handicapping Challenge held Sunday, March 5, 1995 at the TBC Race Centre in your community. In awarding this prize, it is our hope that you will have occasion to visit the Lower Mainland, and Cloverdale Raceway, before next season ends in April 1996.

The enclosure lists the racing dates at Cloverdale Raceway for the balance of the 1994/95 season. This prize is valid through the 1995/96 racing season as well, in the event that you are unable to reserve and visit before this season ends.

When you have selected the date that you and your guest would like to visit the Clubhouse Buffet to partake of your winning dinners, please call or write for reservations to be sure that there is adequate accommodations for you that afternoon or evening. Once that is confirmed, just come to the Raceway on that date and present this letter to the receptionist in the Upper Clubhouse.

Congratulations once again, and be assured that we are looking forward to meeting and hosting you personally as you enjoy a card of live harness racing at Cloverdale Raceway. The marketing team and the Clubhouse staff will do everything possible to make your visit a pleasant and memorable experience.

Yours sincerely,

Bob Groulx
Marketing Manager

HOW TO READ THE RACING FORM

HOW TO READ THE RACING INFORMATION

1	2		
CAM FELLA	N.L.Clements, N.E.Faulkner, JefsRacingStable, Ont., N.J.	Lf. Mid 1 53 M (ft) 4 to 85 $1,746,367	7
	B. r. 6. | (Ml) Most Happy Fella-Nan Cam, by Bret Hanover	85 0 0 0 0 $00	8
10 Pat Crowe, A.(536),160, green, black, white	3 4 5 6 Tr. Pat Crowe	84 0 0 0 0 $00	9

1. CAM FELLA. This is the name of the horse.
2. N. L. CLEMENTS, N. E. FAULKNER, JEFS RACING STABLE, ONT. Owners' name and address.
3. B. r. 6. This indicates the color, sex and age of the horse. Here the "B" is an abbreviation for Bay, "r" means the horse is a ridgling and he is 6 years old.
4. (Mi). This indicates the place of foaling. Cam Fella is a Michigan foal.
5. MOST HAPPY FELLA — NAN CAM, by BRET HANOVER. In order these are the horse's father (sire), Mother (dam), and sire of the dam.
6. TR. PAT CROWE. Pat Crowe trains the horse.
7. Mid. 1:53.1M (ft) 4. This is the best winning time ever for Cam Fella. His life mark was taken at Meadowlands (Mid) in 1:53.1. It is a (M) Mile track and was rated fast. The 4 indicates that his mark was taken as a four-year-old. EARN. TO 85 $1,746,367. This is the record of the total amount he has won in purses to December 31, 1984. His earnings for races since January 1, 1985 are given in the 1985 summary line.
8. 85 0 0 0 0 $00. This is the current summary for Cam Fella. He has yet to race in 1985.
9. 84 0 0 0 0 $00. This is the 1984 summary for Cam Fella. He did not race in 1984.
10. PAT CROWE, A, (536), 160, GREEN, BLACK, WHITE. This is the name of the driver, his class of driving license, his universal driver percentage, weight, and color of his silks. The universal driver percentage is calculated on the number of drives at the current meet. The percentage is current to today's race date.

Date of Race	Year	Track	Race Number	Track Condition	Variant	Condition	Purse	Distance	Leader's Time at %	Leader's Time at %	Leader's Time at %	Winner's Time	Post Position	Pos. and lengths at %	Pos. and lengths at %	Pos. and lengths at %	Pos. and lengths at stretch	Pos. and lengths at finish	Horse's actual time	Dollar odds	Driver	Indiv. time of last %	Winner	Second horse	Third horse	Temperature	Number of starters
Oc22'CM'				ft'	LC		100000	m	28'	57'	1:27'	1:56'	2	1ns	1	1½	1½		1¼	1:58'	'.15	P.Crowe	:29'	CamFella	MillersScout	PerfectOut	14'

Page 2

HOW TO READ THE RACING INFORMATION

CAM FELLA	N.L.Clements, N.E.Faulkner, JefsRacingStable, Ont., N.J.		Lf. Mid	1:53 M (ft) 4	to 85	$1,746,367	7
	B. r. 6. (MI)	Most Happy Fella-Nan Cam, by Bret Hanover	85		0 0 0 0	$00	8
10 Pat Crowe, A.(536),160, green, black, white	3 4 5	6 Tr. Pat Crowe	84		0 0 0 0	$00	9

1. CAM FELLA. This is the name of the horse.
2. N. L. CLEMENTS, N. E. FAULKNER, JEFS RACING STABLE, ONT. Owners' name and address.
3. B. r. 6. This indicates the color, sex and age of the horse. Here the "B" is an abbreviation for Bay, "r" means the horse is a ridgling and he is 6 years old.
4. (MI). This indicates the place of foaling. Cam Fella is a Michigan foal.
5. MOST HAPPY FELLA — NAN CAM, by BRET HANOVER. In order these are the horse's father (sire), Mother (dam), and sire of the dam.
6. TR. PAT CROWE. Pat Crowe trains the horse.
7. Mid. 1:53.1M (ft) 4. This is the best winning time ever for Cam Fella. His life mark was taken at Meadowlands (Mid) in 1:53.1. It is a (M) Mile track and was rated fast. The 4 indicates that his mark was taken as a four-year-old. EARN. TO 85 $1,746,367. This is the record of the total amount he has won in purses to December 31, 1984. His earnings for races since January 1, 1985 are given in the 1985 summary line.
8. 85 0 0 0 0 $00. This is the current summary for Cam Fella. He has yet to race in 1985.
9. 84 0 0 0 0 $00. This is the 1984 summary for Cam Fella. He did not race in 1984.
10. PAT CROWE, A, (536), 160, GREEN, BLACK, WHITE. This is the name of the driver, his class of driving license, his universal driver percentage, weight, and color of his silks. The universal driver percentage is calculated on the number of drives at the current meet. The percentage is current to today's race date.

Date of Race	Oc22'CM'
Year	
Track	
Race Number	n'
Track Condition	LC
Variant	
Condition	
Purse	100000
Distance	m .28'
Leader's Time at ¼	.57'
Leader's Time at ½	1:27"
Leader's Time at ¾	1:56'
Winner's Time	
Post Position	2
Pos. and lengths at ¼	1ᵐ
Pos. and lengths at ½	1'
Pos. and lengths at ¾	1'½
Pos. and lengths at stretch	1'¾
Pos. and lengths at finish	1'
Horse's actual time	1:56'
Dollar odds	*.15
Driver	P.Crowe
Indiv. time of last ¼	.29'
Winner	CamFella
Second horse	MillersScout
Third horse	PerfectOut
Temperature	14'
Number of starters	

EQUIPMENT

Through casual observation, I have noticed many people buying their racing forms at the gate. I do not recommend this for our system. I cannot do a thorough job handicapping between races. Many people do not even have pens, and to me, this is unworkable and ineffective. I save all my racing forms and file them in order in a three-ring binder. This is for future reference, so that when I come across a horse I do not remember thoroughly I can look up his previous record in a few seconds. I keep my racing forms for two complete seasons.

<u>NECESSARY EQUIPMENT</u>

    a. Racing form (bought in advance and studied)
    b. Pen (preferably with two or three different colors)
    c. Binder (for filing old race forms)

WHY A SYMBOL METHOD?

All systems use some method of isolating, evaluating, and marking important information. One technique uses a plus/minus evaluation for different important statistics. Another technique uses abbreviations such as FR - Front Runner; C - Closer; and so on.

KLEIN'S HANDICAPPING SYSTEM uses a <u>SYMBOL METHOD</u>. There are major advantages to using symbols. First of all, you create a mental image, like a picture, of how the race will unfold. Second, your racing form is full of letters and numbers, so adding more of the same can compound the confusion. Remember, we are trying to simplify the process. Symbols are in direct contrast to the other information in your racing form. You can see quickly and clearly the decisions you have made, while doing your handicapping.

GROUNDWORK

GROUNDWORK consists of <u>ten preliminary steps</u> that must be completed before you decide on your <u>Contenders</u> or <u>Non-Contenders</u>. We suggest you complete each step individually for all the horses in a race before going on to the next category.

<u>GROUND WORK</u> is divided into two categories:

MAIN GROUND WORK

All the categories in the Main Ground Work are of equal importance. I have put them in my own order of importance. These categories must be checked, evaluated and marked. They are:

    a. Date
    b. Driver or Jockey
    c. Class
    d. Speed
    e. Running Style

Comments and explanations of these categories will follow.

SECONDARY GROUND WORK

    a. Track Condition
    b. Horses in Trouble
    c. Difficult Posts
    d. Winning Percentage
    e. Big Moves During Race

Comments and explanations of these categories will follow.

All of the <u>GROUND WORK</u> has to be completed before you eliminate any horse. When you have finished all the Ground Work, you will have a clear mental picture of <u>each</u> horse in the race. Only then are you ready to make an evaluation on the horses you do not consider contenders.

TO PRACTICE COSTS ONLY THE PRICE OF A RACING FORM AND YOUR SPARE TIME.

EXPLANATION OF SYMBOLS USED IN MAIN GROUND WORK

<u>MAIN GROUND WORK</u> (See "SAMPLE RACE" - for illustrations of all the following symbols)

<u>DATE</u>

If the horse is running on a regular basis (once every 13 days or less) we mark a diagonal line through the horse's previous racing dates.

If the horse has had 14 days or more off, without a race, we mark a line at the date and write down how long the break was. This is marked in red, to draw attention to it.

IF A HORSE HAS BEEN OFF FOR 14 DAYS OR MORE WE USUALLY GIVE HIM ONE RACE AFTER THE REST BEFORE WE CONSIDER HIM.

Standardbred horses usually race every seven to 14 days. If they have taken off more time than this, there must be some reason they are not racing. We would then be suspicious of their condition, and especially so if they were running poorly before the time off, or if they were vet scratched prior to their time off. Checking the date and seeing if the horse has been running regularly or has had time off is <u>extremely important</u> in our system. It should take about one minute to check and mark the date category.

<u>DRIVER</u>

We use two symbols to mark Driver Changes. If the driver is the same as in the last race e use this symbol **V** . If there is a change in drivers we use this symbol ◯ in red. If we determine it is a positive change of driver we add a plus sign in the circle, like this ⊕ . If we determine it a negative driver change, then we add a minus sign to the circle, like this ⊖. All these symbols should be marked in the driver's column of the racing form. It should take you about 30 seconds to make these checks and symbols.

You can determine if a driver change is positive or negative by checking the driver standings in your form.

At this point, you may feel that all this seems fairly trivial, but be patient, for the overall picture on your racing form will be <u>clear</u> and <u>unforgettable</u>.

CLASS

We have two methods of determining Class:

    a. Judge class by purse: If a horse was racing for a purse of $1,800.00 and today is running for a purse of $1,700.00, we consider him dropping in class.

    a. Judge class by: Checking the <u>Class column</u> or <u>Type of Race</u> at the top of each race. If today's horse is competing in a $10,000 claiming race, but last race out was in an $8,000 claiming race, then this horse is moving up.

TRY TO DETERMINE AT WHAT LEVEL THE HORSE WAS COMPETITIVE.

There are three symbols for marking the Class:

1) A horse staying at the same class level is marked like this

2) A horse that is moving up in class is marked like this

3) A horse that is moving down in class is marked (in red) like this

<u>SPEED</u>

We judge the speed of a horse by taking the fastest time in his last showing races. We only use a time if he was within three lengths or less of the winner. To better judge a horse, we also observe his fastest winning time last year. We circle our fastest times in red.

EXPLANATION OF COMPUTED TIMES

A horse's speed will vary, in a one-mile race, at different size tracks. The reason for this variation is:

To run a one-mile race at a mile track the horse runs around two turns. At a five-eighths mile track, the horse runs around three turns. At a half mile track, the horse runs around four turns.

If a horse is from a track of a different size than today's, then by adding or subtracting the appropriate seconds you will be able to better assess his speed. We call this a computed time. An example is:

The horse runs 2:00 at a mile track; he will run approximately 2:01 at a five eighths mile track, and approximately 2:04 at a half mile track.

RUNNING STYLE

The running style of an individual horse is extremely important in our system. If a horse shows he is determined to get to the front, or very close to the front, from any post, we use this symbol to indicate so: This means he likes to stay close to the speed or on the front, and we call him a Front Runner. If a horse likes to come from off the pace, we use this symbol to indicate so: This means he is a Closer. We mark these symbols on the extreme right-hand side of each horse's previous races.

If you cannot figure out what running style a horse has, he is probably running poorly. In this case it is extremely important to look him up in your earlier racing forms, which you have saved, to determine his running style.

EXPLANATION OF SYMBOLS USED IN SECONDARY GROUND WORK

SECONDARY GROUND WORK (See "SAMPLE RACE"
- for illustrations of all the following symbols)

TRACK CONDITION

Be sure to check the track condition for previous races. Maybe your horse has had a stretch of bad tracks. If the track is off today, check to see how he performed on tracks.

HORSES IN TROUBLE

This category is very important, and requires close attention. If a horse was interfered with, it must be marked. If a horse has run outside (parked) for half the race or more, it must be brought to your attention. If your horse has broken equipment or if he was boxed in, or if he broke stride, or if he had to run two or three horses wide, all these instances should be drawn to your attention. We do this by circling the infractions in red.

DIFFICULT POSTS

If a horse had post positions 5, 6 or 7, they should be circled in red. These posts are much more difficult to win from, and the driver usually has to contend with more traffic, requiring much greater driving skill.

WINNING PERCENTAGE

Many times a horse will have a much greater winning percentage than his competitors. Observing this can be an important point in your handicapping evaluation. We also observe lifetime winnings. The more money a horse has won, the more experience he has at winning.

BIG MOVES DURING RACE

This maneuver can sometimes be easily overlooked. A horse may have made up many lengths in any area of the race and then finished poorly. In making what we call this "big move," he may have exerted too much energy, therefore the poor finish. Next time, if he is paced better, or has better racing luck, he would be a definite contender. This is often an indication of a horse coming into good form. We mark this, in red, with a straight line in the area of the race where it happened.

MARKING AREAS • • • MAIN GROUND WORK
Date
Class
Speed
Driver
Running Style
Difficult Posts
Horses in Trouble
• •
Big Moves
Track Condition
Winnings
MARKING AREAS • • • SECONDARY GROUND WORK
7

PUTTING THE SYMBOL TECHNIQUE INTO PRACTICE

We will handicap the six races for the March 12, 1986 Cloverdale Racing Card, in Cloverdale, British Columbia, Canada. We are playing the SuperSix and are concerned with races three through eight. This was a winning card for us, so we can show you firsthand how our handicapping worked. We can show how a small wager can translate into a handsome profit.

We use the Symbol Technique for handicapping Thoroughbred as well as Standardbred racing. Of course, there are some important differences: in thoroughbred racing, for instance, there is a jockey instead of a driver; the post position is of less importance; and a jockey's weight allowance is of major importance. There are more horses in a Thoroughbred race but there's no such thing as breaking stride, as found in Standardbred racing. Most of the changes, however, deal with common sense. It is important to realize that our Main and Secondary Ground Work formats are the same for both types of racing. We have been equally successful in Thoroughbred as well as Standardbred racing.

PLEASE READ THE FOLLOWING PAGES CAREFULLY TO UNDERSTAND HOW THE CATEGORIES OF THE MAIN AND SECONDARY GROUND WORK ARE APPLIED TO YOUR RACING FORM.

When you have finished studying each race we have handicapped, check the race results on page 15. Take note of how each horse raced. Who went to the front, who closed, and who did nothing. If you practice this technique you will be amazed at how accurately you can predict how the race will unfold.

THE FOLLOWING ARE ALL STANDARDBRED RACES.

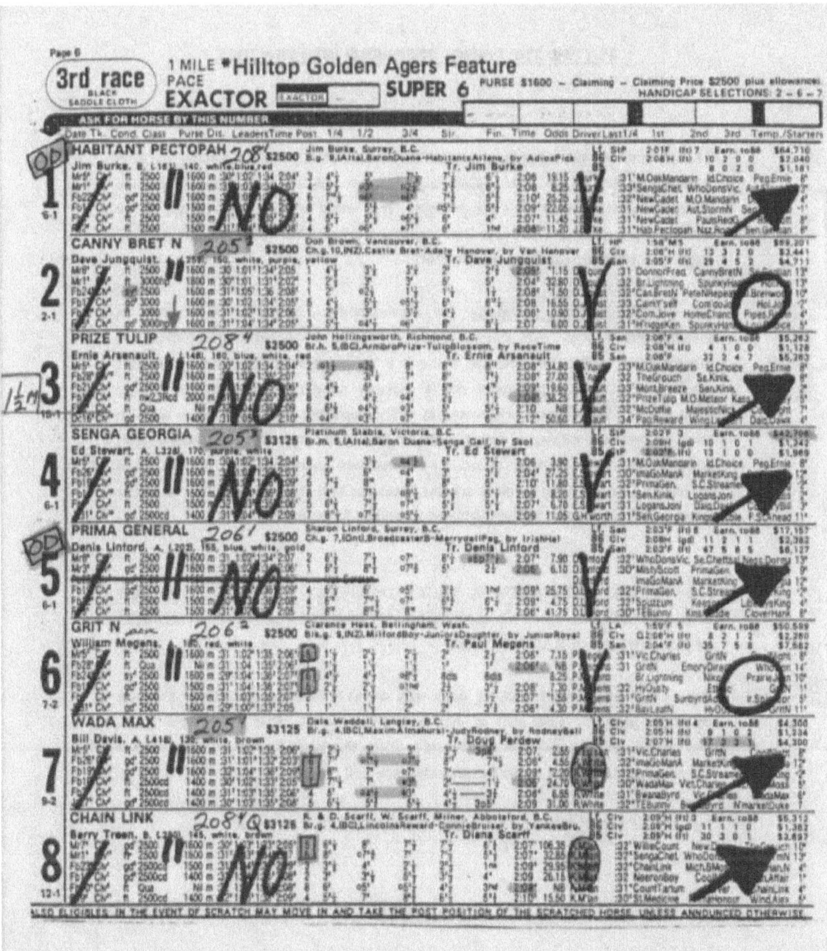

* Draw a line through the dates of all vet scratches - example No. 5 in this race.

* O'D next to the horse's No. means the horse is owned and driven by same family (anothter positive point if he is a Contender today).

* I use the space after the horse's name to display his speed rating. Fastest speed ratings are marked in red.

RACE #3

(START OF SUPER 6)

MAIN GROUND WORK

Date

All have been racing on a regular basis.

Driver

The driver changes on [7 and $8 are both positive driver changes. When you glance down the driver column you see the changes clearly.

Class

The whole field raced at the same level the last out but #2 dropped a notch, to today's level, on February 24th he had the best post and he won in the slop.

Speed

No. 7 has the fastest winning time of $2:05^1$

No. 2 and No. 4 were tied for second at $2:05^3$.

Running Style

No. 2 and No. 6 appear to like the front, and that seems to be the extent of the challenge for the lead.

No. 7 came from well off the pace on February 10th, from the same post as toda . He went 3 wide at the three-quarter pole and won handily with a $2:05^1$ time. He appears to be our strongest Closer.

SECONDARY GROUND WORK

KLEIN'S HANDICAPPING SYSTEMS

Track Condition

All tracks were fast or good in the last couple of outings.

Horses in Trouble

No. 4 was in contention but was boxed in.

No. 7 was disqualified from third to last in his last race.

Difficult Posts

No. 7 has had three out of four difficult posts, but seems to do well from the back.

No. 8 has had two tough posts since his win.

Winning Percentage

No. 4 as a five-year-old mare has earned $42,706.00.

Big Moves

No. 7 closed 12-3/4 lengths on February 10th. He went from seventh by 11-1/2 to first by 1-1/4. In the last quarter he went 3 wide and closed 6-1/4 lengths. This is a good example of a big move.

SUMMARY

Now that we have completed our Main and Secondary Ground Work we will comment on our final decisions. First I eliminate "non-contenders" so I don't waste any more time on them.

NON-CONTENDERS

No. 1 has had decent posts, is staying at the same class level and is showing nothing. I write a big "NO" on the left.

No. 3 is slow and is finishing well back.

No. 4 boxed in last out but has been well back pass on him today.

No. 5 broke stride when not in contention.

No. 8 is very slow and shows no sign of life last two races.

CONTENDERS

No. 2 has a good post for his front running style and his last effort was a good one. He was racing with a notch better and he's as fast as any here.

No. 6 has been racing very well, but with his front running style and having to compete with No. 2, who is also a Front Runner, the six post should cost him today. No. 7 is a very strong Closer and seems to do well from the back posts, so the No. 7 post doesn't hinder him. He has a positive driver change to Davis and has the fastest time of $2:05^{1}$.

We are betting the SuperSix, so we select two horses in this more difficult, unpredictable race. They are No. 2, our Front Runner, and No. 7, our Closer.

* Race No. 4 - a good example of a variety of sexes and ages.

* We subtract 2 seconds from qualifying times, for a truer indication of how fast the horse can race.

* Horses No. 4, No. 5, and No. 7 are racing so poorly we have to leave their running styles unmarked.

RACE #4

<u>**MAIN GROUND WORK**</u>

Date

All qualify.

Driver

No. I is back to his regular driver.

No. 6 has a probational driver which we see as negative.

Class

All are equal, non-winners lifetime.

Speed

Since these are non-winners lifetime, we do not have too much to go on, so we take their times from good Qualifiers and previous races where they finished reasonably well.

No. I has a $2:09^2$, and is our third fastest time.

No. 3 has a good Qualifier on February 21st at $2:07^4$, and is our second fastest time.

No. 8 was in contention in the last quarter of the March 8th race but broke stride in the stretch. After the break she was pulled up and still finished third, 4-3/4 lengths behind the winner. Because of her problems we will accept her $2:06^3$ as a legitimate time.

Running Style

No. I appears to like the front.

No. 3 off his February 21st Qualifier appears to close.

No. 8 appears to close well.

<u>SECONDARY GROUND WORK</u>

Track Condition

No. 5 had a very sloppy track last out.

Horses in Trouble

No. 5 had a break at the start.

No. 8 had a break at the finish.

Difficult Posts

No. 2 had the 6 post in his last Qualifier.

Winning Percentage

No. I with $2,336.00 tops the field.

Big Moves

No. 6 and No. 8 have notable moves indicated by red lines.

ROBERT KLEIN

SUMMARY

NON-CONTENDERS

No. 2 is slow and finished well back and has a B Class driver.

No. 4 finished well back from better posts than today's.

No. 5 has a tendency to break stride.

No. 6 has a probational driver, has slow times and a difficult post today. No. 7 has 25 races and no wins, and with today's tough post is a noncontender.

CONTENDERS

No. I gives consistent efforts and has a good post today for his running style.

No. 3 is strictly a long shot because we like his February 21st Qualifier. No. 8 is our fastest horse and has an excellent post for a Closer.

Here we selected three horses, because racing at this level is very inconsistent. They are No. I, No. 3, and No. 8.

* You may feel: "What's the sense in writing down each horse's time when they are all just a fraction of a second apart?" Here's your answer: Every 1/5 of a second is equal to 1 length. Often the winner of a race is decided by a camera, so you can see how important a fraction of a second becomes.

* 1 second is equal to 5 lengths (standard in harness racing).

RACE #5

MAIN GROUND WORK

Date

No. 4 off four months.

No. 6 was off 16 days.

No. 7 was off 24 days prior to March 5th.

Driver

No. 2 went back to his regular driver.

Class

No. I and No. 4 are moving up in class.

No. 5, No. 6, and No. 7 are dropping in class.

Speed

No. 2 has a $2:03^2$.

No. 5 has a $2:03^4$.

No. 6 is our fastest horse with a $2:02^2$. (computed)

Running Style

No. I, No. 4, No. 5, and No. 7 are all Front Runners.

No. 2 and No. 6 are the Closers.

SECONDARY GROUND WORK

Track Condition

No. 6 had two out of four sloppy tracks.

Horses in Trouble

Nil

Difficult Posts

Nil

Winning Percentage

No. I - 31 starts; 13 wins for $10,000 (must have won at lower levels).

No. 2 is having a great season with 10 out of I l in the money.

No. 6 - 38 starts; 10 wins for $27,000 (a great record).

Big Moves

No. 2 closes well.

SUMMARY

NON-CONTENDERS

No. I is moving up in class and could not win with lesser.

No. 4 was off four months, and is moving up in class.

No. 5 was claimed March 1st, and had a dismal effort for his new owners. No. 7 finishing far back from good posts.

All of these non-contenders get a big "NO" so we do not spend any more time studying them.

CONTENDERS

No. 2 has won twice at this level, and has a good 1986 record.

No. 6 is a classic example of the benefit of filing old racing forms. The running style of No. 6 appears as a Front Runner, but he only front runs from front posts. In a case like this, you need to look up additional races so you can evaluate his running style when the horse is RACING WELL. Upon checking, this horse proves to be a Closer. Why the horse was not raced for 16 days is a negative to us. We would usually pass on him except for his last good effort in the slop. The last factor in our decision is that there were only six horses left after the scratch, and four of them appeared to like the front; this should set up a good Closer. Also, No. 6 is our fastest horse.

Our choices in the fifth are No. 2 and No. 6.

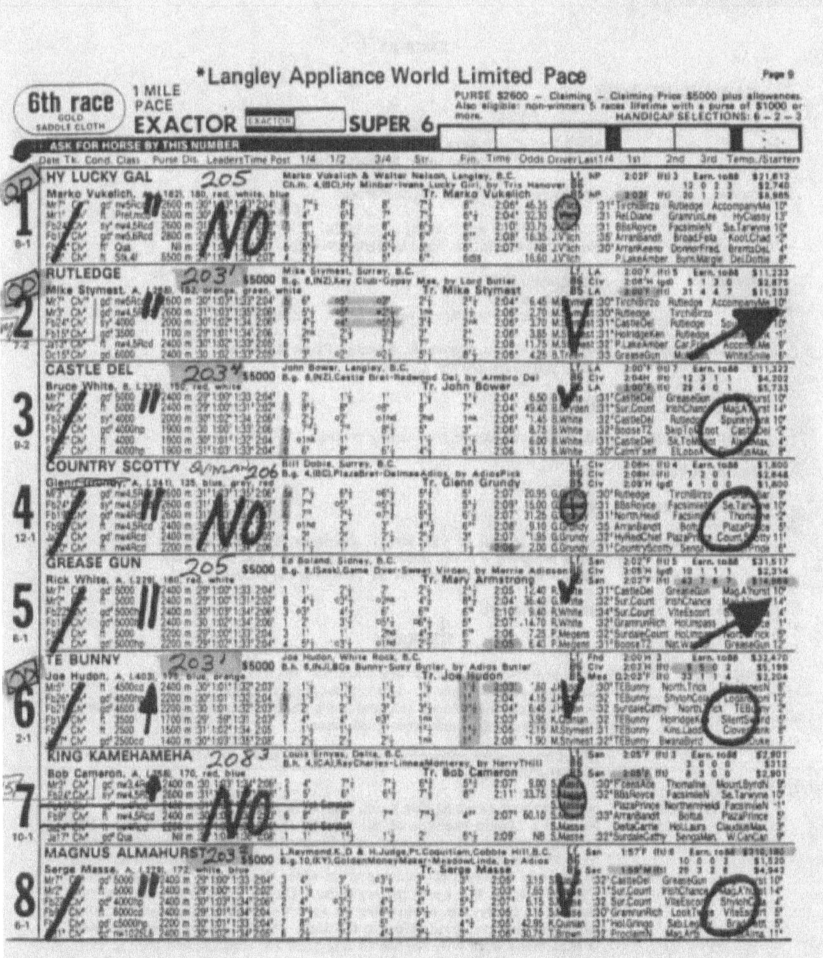

*   In Standardbred racing, males and females are considered equal.

RACE #6

MAIN GROUND WORK

Date

No. 7 run two races since his vet scratch.

Driver

No. I has a negative driver change.

No. 4 has a positive driver change.

No. 7 has a negative driver change.

Class

No. 6 is moving up a notch, and the rest are staying at the same level.

Speed

No. 2 has a $2:03^1$ (computed winning time last year).

No. 3 has a $2:03^4$ (computed winning time last year).

No. 6 has a $2:03^1$ winning time last out.

Running Style

No. 3, No. 4, No. 6, and No. 8 are all Front Runners.

No. 2 and No. 5 are Closers.

SECONDARY GROUND WORK

Track Condition

KLEIN'S HANDICAPPING SYSTEMS

All equal.

Horses in Trouble

No. 2 ran outside for half the race in his last three outings.

No. 4 broke stride at the start last out.

Difficult Posts

We note No. 3 did well from difficult posts.

No. 4 has had tough posts his last three.

No. 6 did extremely well from difficult posts.

Winning Percentage

No. 5 had a great year in 1985.

No. 6 won five of last six (very impressive).

We note that No. 8 is ten years old, and has career earnings of $210,000.

Big Moves

No. 2 closed 6-3/4 lengths last out.

SUMMARY

NON-CONTENDERS

No. I is running poorly; has a negative driver change.

No. 4 broke last out and is slow.

No. 5 finishing well back, with even better posts than today's.

No. 7 has had two vet scratches within his last six races, finishing well back; is slow and has a tough post today.

No. 8 is fading and not making a move, with good posts - his condition is suspect.

CONTENDERS

No. 2 is a good strong Closer, and is tied for our fastest speed rating. He is also owner-driven.

No. 3 won easily last out, and is reasonably fast.

No. 6 is moving up a notch, and has a tough post for his front running style, but it is hard to go against a horse that has won five out of his last six starts. He is also owner-driven, and is tied for our fastest time.

We have selected two horses here. They are No. 2 (our Closer) and No. 6 (our strongest Front Runner). We would like to have taken three horses, but to keep our bet price down we had to let one of our Front Runners go. No. 3 was slower than No. 6, so we went with our fastest horses.

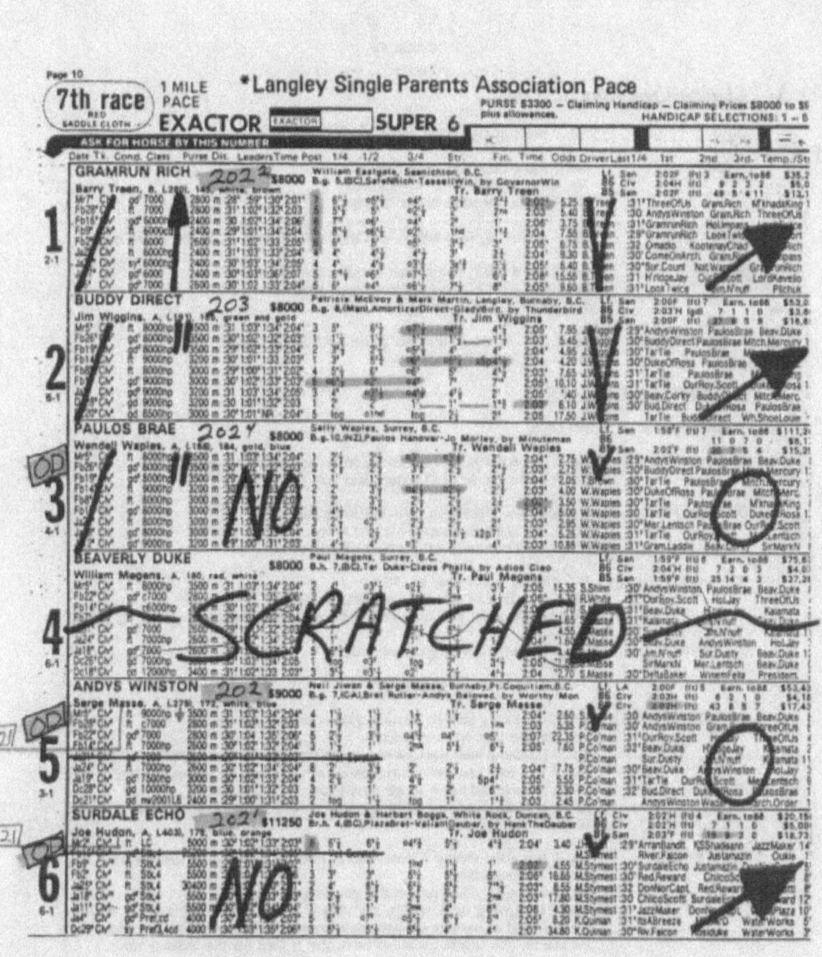

* If a horse finishes within three lengths of the winner, do not eliminate him unless you have a good reason.

RACE #7

<u>MAIN GROUND WORK</u>

Date

No. 5 won his third and fourth races after being off 21 days.

No. 6 has run once since being off three weeks.

Driver

No changes.

Class

No. 1 is moving up a notch.

No. 5 is dropping a notch, after a win.

Speed

No. 5 has a 2:02 last year.

No. 6 has a $2:02^1$ from a front post.

We consider the whole field completely equal in speed.

Running Style

No. 3 and No. 5 are Front Runners.

No. 1 and No. 2 are Closers.

<u>SECONDARY GROUND WORK</u>

Track Condition

Not significant.

Horses in Trouble

No. 2 has had problems in three out of the last six starts. He was boxed in his last race.

No. 3 was boxed-in his last.

Difficult Posts

No. I had 5 tough posts his last 5 races. No. 6 gets another tough post today.

Winning Percentage

No. 2 won about 25% of his starts last year.

No. 3 won about 25% of his starts last year.

No. 6 won 67% of his starts last year.

Big Moves

No. 2 pulled away on December 28th to win by 5-3/4 lengths, and on February 26th he won by 2-1/2 at the same level.

SUMMARY

NON-CONTENDERS

No. I was winning at two notches lower; he is a Closer in a front running post.

No. 5 won with a slow time on a fast track, and is a strong Front Runner with a tough post today.

No. 6 has had a three-week rest, and because of today's difficult post we will pass on him.

CONTENDERS

No. 3 is actually a strong contender, and we are gambling by not taking him today, but we do not like this driver, and for that reason alone will pass on him. Knowing your drivers or jockeys at your particular track can sometimes be your deciding factor.

No. 2 has won at a notch higher, by 5-3/4 lengths with a respectable 2:03. He has had many traffic problems between wins. We call this horse an on-pace Closer. This means he can run a few lengths behind the lead and still have a good finishing kick. This is the main reason he has so many traffic problems. When it is time for him to make his move, the lead horses are slowing up while the back horses are closing; hence there are horses all around him. With today's small field, he will have more of an advantage, as he will have less traffic.

We are taking No. 2 as a single selection. He has won handily at a notch higher and at this same level. We realize that any one of these horses can win on a given day. The difference may be a better driver, a more suitable post for a particular running style, or maybe just better racing luck.

Notice in the race results that he has the longest odds of the field.

KLEIN'S HANDICAPPING SYSTEMS

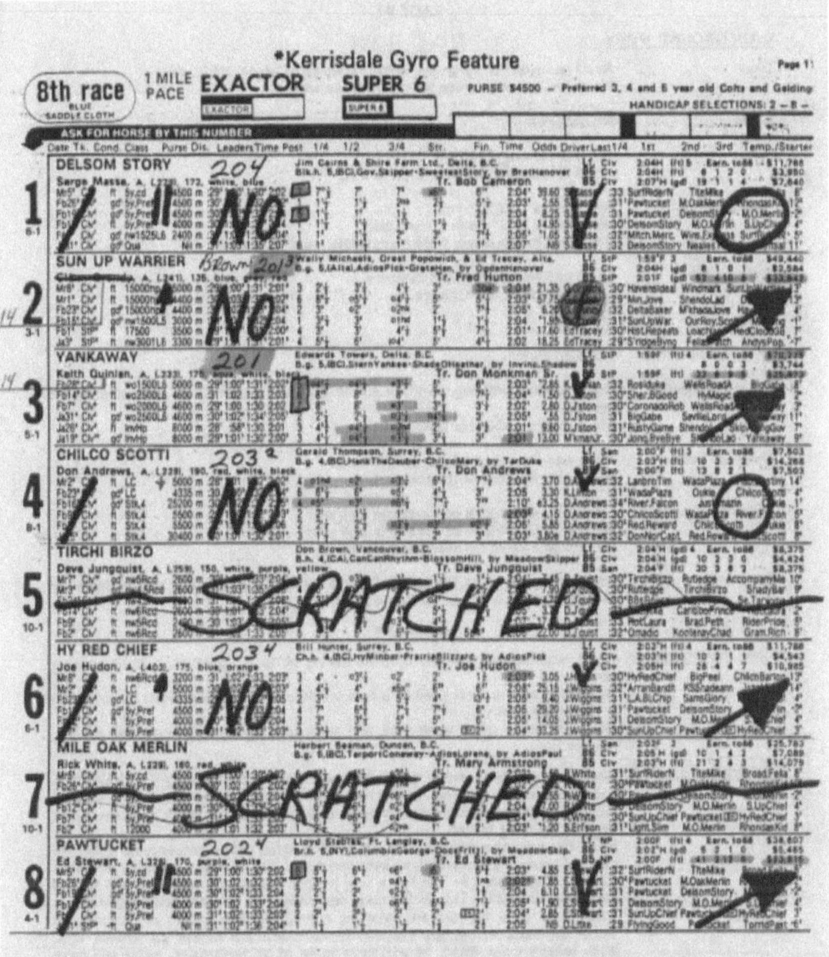

* Do your handicapping before you get to the track, to avoid distractions. Other jobs need your attention; e.g., driver changes, late scratches, and draw-in horses have to be evaluated.

RACE #8

MAIN GROUND WORK

Date

No. 3 raced once after 14 days off.

Driver

No. 2 has a positive driver change.

Class

No. 2 is moving up from the claiming ranks.

No. 3 is dropping down after doing well in the Invitationals on January 19th and 26th.

No. 4 is dropping.

No. 6 is moving up, after his win.

Speed

No. 3 had a 2:01 on January 19th, finishing third, our fastest horse.

No. 2 had a $2:01^3$ to be within one length of winner his last out. No other horses have 2:01s in their time column.

Running Style

No. I and No. 4 are Front Runners.

No. 2, No. 3, No. 6, and No. 8 are Closers.

SECONDARY GROUND WORK

KLEIN'S HANDICAPPING SYSTEMS

Track Condition

All have fast tracks last out.

Horses in Trouble

No. I broke stride when not in contention.

No. 2 had broken equipment.

No. 3 ran 2 wide the first half, then went 3 wide for the last 1/4.

No. 4 ran outside the entire race.

No. 8 was interfered with in the stretch.

Difficult Posts

No. I has had two tough posts his last three starts.

No. 3 has had three difficult posts his last three races.

Winning Percentage

No. 2 had a good year in 1985.

No. 3 has a good winning percentage; has earned $70,000, which is the most for all these horses.

No. 8 was 50% in the money in 1985.

Big Moves

No. 3 closed 5-3/4 lengths on February 7th, in the last 1/4, at a 2:02[1].

SUMMARY

NON-CONTENDERS

No. I broke stride his last out, and is slow.

No. 2 is moving up from claiming ranks and not winning.

No. 4 has a suspect driver up, who seems to get his horses into many traffic problems. Finished poorly last out after front running entire race from same post as today's. He tends to fade.

No. 6 is moving up too much, and moves to a much more difficult post.

CONTENDERS

No. 3 has had one outing since his two-week break. He showed much stamina on February 28th. He's our fastest horse and our biggest money winner at this age. We like the driver change and the better post, and with a closing type of running style we feel No. 3 has a good shot from this position.

No. 8 has a nice strong closing finish and today is moving to a better post after having an interference in his last. He looks good, but does show only a $2:02^4$, which works out to about nine lengths slower than No. 3.

Therefore (again to keep the price of our bet down), we will select only one horse in this race. He is No. 3. He is fast, he has class, he is dropping, and he has a good post for his running style. With so much going for him he is hard to count out, and with a dash of racing luck we will have our winner!

Notice in the race results that all the horses had some interference. This was a result of broken equipment on No. 2. Fortunately, our horse cleared the trouble and won easily. Maybe most of the credit can go to Yankaway's new driver for the last two races.

NOW THAT YOU HAVE GONE THROUGH THE SIX RACES STEP BY STEP, YOU CAN APPRECIATE THAT IT IS NOT SO DIFFICULT. MOST OF THE WINNERS HAD EITHER THE FASTEST WINNING TIMES OR WERE HORSES THAT HAD TROUBLE IN THEIR LAST OUT: THREE OF THE WINNERS WERE HOT FAVORITES; TWO HORSES HAD TROUBLE LAST OUT (NO. 7 IN THE THIRD RACE AND NO. 2 IN THE SEVENTH); THE TOUGHEST PICK WAS THE FIFTH RACE WITH MULTI RAINBOW. IF 1 HAD NOT KEPT MY OLD FORMS TO LOOK UP HIS RUNNING STYLE, 1 PROBABLY WOULD NOT HAVE SELECTED HIM.

THERE WERE 23,000 BETS MADE THIS NIGHT, SO IMAGINE: WE HAD THE ONLY CORRECT COMBINATION WITH OUR $24 INVESTMENT A RETURN OF $17,931.

RACE RESULTS

CLOVERDALE RACEWAY CHARTS — Charts for March 12, 1986 — Attendance 2491 — Handle $397816 — Temp. 7

First Race — Purse $1500 — Claiming $2500 (NW in 1986) — m — h

EL LOBO A · STRANGE MAGE · JUST DUKE · BI CH · RAILOAD TAM · CESPOOL · SHADOW'S DAUNTLESS · DELANEY

Mutual Prices 3.66 3.60 3.20 · 7.10 3.20 2.90 · Quinella 1-4 pays $15.30

Second Race — Purse $1500 — Claiming $2500 — m — h

WILLIE COUNT · VICTOR CHARLES · DANTE SPECIAL · SUP DEL BOB · MILE OAK MANDARIN · SHYLOH PIPER · NIXON · LOGANS JONI

Mutual Prices 16.10 3.70 3.30 · 2.60 2.90 5.10 · Exactor 8-1 pays $15.90

Daily Double 1-8 pays $13.30 · Willie Count Lifemark 2.06 1h.7

Third Race — Purse $1500 — Claiming $2500 — m — h

WADA MAI · SENGA GEORGIA · CANNY BRET N · PREE TULIP · GRIT N · CHAIN LINK · PRIMA GENERAL · HABITANT PECTOFAN

Mutual Prices 16.50 10.50 3.60 · 10.50 4.00 3.60 · Exactor 7-4 pays $99.40

Fourth Race — Purse $1600 — 3yo younger NW3R — m — h

RICHLAND FERN · RESORT · CLOVER ON THE HILL · DELTA DIAMOND · DOLLCIAM MAJOR · N.A. CONTENDER · RENDAL MIST · WHIPPER SONG

Mutual Prices 6.20 3.00 2.60 · 3.80 2.40 3.20 · Exactor 8-1 pays $14.00

Richland Fern Lifemark 2.07 4H.4

Fifth Race — Purse $1500 — Claiming Hdcp $3000-$3500 — m — h

BOTTOME · *vet scratch* · MULTI RAINBOW · HOLRIDGE KEN · KREIOUS DUFF · SPLASH HANE · J.B MONACO · SNOOPY DIRECT

Mutual Prices 15.60 4.40 3.40 · 2.60 2.40 4.80 · Exactor 5-3 pays $39.10

Kreious Duke Claimed by A.Cooper,D.C.Smith.

Sixth Race — Purse $2600 — Claiming $5000-AE NY5R — m — h

TE BUNNY · CASTLE DEL · RUTLEDGE · GREASE GUN · HY LUCKY GAL · COUNTRY SCOTTY · MAGNUS ALMAHURST · KING KAMEHAMEHA

Mutual Prices 4.10 2.90 2.30 · 3.40 2.40 3.30 · Exactor 6-3 pays $14.10

Seventh Race — Purse $3300 — Claiming Hdcp $4000-$5000 — m — h

BEAVERLY DUKE · *vet scratch* · BUDDY DIRECT · SURDALE ECHO · ANDYS WINSTON · PHLEOS MAAI · GHAMRUN RICH

Mutual Prices 11.10 4.60 3.60 · 6.30 3.80 4.30 · Exactor 2-4 pays $63.30

Eighth Race — Purse $4500 — Preferred 3,4,5yo colts & geldings — m — h

SUN UP WARMER · TRICK BINZO · *vet scratch* · MILE OAK MERLIN · *vet scratch* · TAMARANT · CHILCO SCOTTI · PAWTUCKET · HY RED CHIEF · DELSION STORY

Mutual Prices 4.20 3.60 3.70 · 11.80 6.70 3.00 · Exactor 3-4 pays $45.20

Super Six 7-6-6-6-3-3 pays $17931.15

Ninth Race — Purse $2200 — NW3Races-AE NW3RLWL6 — m — h

RACING GLORY · HY STED GENE · PAC MAN DEAN · SURDALE EDDY · WINSOME AGAIN · KAMEANA · KONTIKI AL · NORTHERN SCOOTER

Mutual Prices $7.00 20.70 9.90 · 9.10 4.60 5.20 · Exactor 3-9 pays $562.00

Racing Glory Lifemark 2.06 4H.5

Tenth Race — Purse $1500 — Claiming $2500 (NWVL6) — m — h

KEVIN MINBAR · *vet scratch* · TUATAN RIDGE · ZERRO N · SEAVERA CLEO · KEESNO · ANTIQUE DUSTY · CASH INVESTMENT · FORT LINCOLN · CLAUDIUS MAXMUS

Mutual Prices 12.00 4.80 4.10 · 4.30 3.40 8.50 · Triactor 9-3-2 pays $669.80

SUMMARY

We have handicapped the six races for the Super Six on March 12, 1986. Let's focus on what we have learned.

By completing the ten steps in the Ground Work, which should take you approximately 15 minutes, you will now have a <u>visual</u> record on your racing form of what each horse is doing. At this point a mental image of how it will unfold begins to emerge. You will see which horses do not qualify in the date category. Your Driver changes will be noted and not forgotten. In the Class department you can see immediately who is dropping, staying the same, or moving up. The Speed of each horse will be easily comparable and you can see at a glance who is the fastest, second fastest and so on. Having determined the Running Style of each horse, you have now created a "mental image" of the entire race. In our opinion, this is extremely important. The better you are at predicting the strategy of each horse and driver combination, the more successful you will be.

SETTING UP THE RACE

Let's use Race #5 as our example. It has six horses; four of them are Front

Runners, two are Closers. I imagine the race to unfold in this manner; The four Front Runners will be pushing each other to gain the lead and in doing so they may expend too much energy early in the race, not leaving enough for the finish. While the Front Runners are battling it out, the Closers will be conserving energy by staying back. When it comes time for the Closers to make their move, you should have a front group that is tiring while the back group should still have a burst of conserved energy. If you check the results of Race #5, you will see how horses No. I, No. 2, and No. 4 stayed close for the first half. At this point No. I was expended and No. 2 and No. 4 continued to battle. In the meantime No. 6, who had been coasting along at the back of the pack, started his closing move at the 3/4 pole, and made up 5 1/2 lengths in the last quarter to win by a comfortable 2 1/2 lengths. IN SETTING UP A RACE, INCLUDE ALL THE HORSES, CONTENDERS AND NON-CONTENDERS.

You must include the non-contenders even though they should not be a factor at the finish. If they are Front Runners they will still challenge for the lead no matter what their form. They may only last for part of the race but that may be enough to bring added pressure on your Front Running contender.

CONTENDERS AND MAKING YOUR FINAL DECISIONS

By now you should have looked over the whole race and come to some conclusions as to which horse or horses have a real chance at winning. But what happens if you end up with three or four possible contenders? How are you going to do your final processing so you can make a real bet with only one or two choices? Here are some key points to look for to determine your best contenders. If your horse:

a. has the fastest speed rating

b. has won at today's class level

c. has won his last race handily (by two or more lengths) even though he is moving up a class level or two. He will be very competitive again, as he is in good form.

d. was in contention in his last, but had traffic problems, was boxed in, ran wide for half the race or more, had broken equipment, etc.

e. is the only Front Runner from any post, and is equally competitive in the speed department. He will get the lead and will be hard to catch.

f. if all the speeds vary only fractionally, then we would consider which ones are: dropping in class, have better posts for their running style, have the leading driver or a positive driver change or have had trouble last out.

<u>HOW TO SPOT UNUSUAL SITUATIONS</u>

a. If a horse was claimed and is dropping for his next outing, he should be a good bet, because, after all, who would risk having his horse claimed again, for less money, unless he thought he had a good chance at picking up the win purse? Yes, it does happen!

b. When Front Runners greatly outnumber the Closers, carefully check your fastest and best Closer.

c. When a horse is staying exactly at the same level for many races in a row. If he shows any sign of improvement, consider him carefully next time.

d. If a horse is being claimed and then reclaimed by his original owner, consider him carefully. This horse could run poorly for his new connections, but could improve immediately for his old barn, with whom he is familiar.

Once you have your contenders, you are in the final stage of making your selections. Now each individual must rely on his own personal interpretation. Try not to let sentimentality cloud your educated decisions. We have missed out on very large wins because of making a sentimental choice.

We hope the information in KLEIN'S HANDICAPPING SYSTEMS will shed some new light on this most challenging, rewarding and enjoyable sport. We do not profess to know all the answers, but we've shared what we do know with you. If you have any questions or would like to share some of your experiences with us, we would be most happy to hear from you.

Klein's Handicapping Systems

If you wish to purchase additional copies or would like to recommend our system to a friend, please feel free to do so. Thank you.

About the Author

Robert Klein, his wife Aagje and their dog Nova bet the horse race tracks together. Never having taken thoroughbred and standardbred racing seriously, everything changed when the tracks came up with a new bet. The sweep six. At that point they passionately picked up on the new betting options. After winning many sweep sixes they decided to share their strategies with others. And they have now published how-to guidelines for other racetrack enthusiasts.